NASCAR Training Ground

Gail Blasser Riley
AR B.L.: 3.2
Points: 0.5   MG

The World of NASCAR

NASCAR Training Ground

by Gail Blasser Riley

Reading Consultant:
Barbara J. Fox
Reading Specialist
North Carolina State University

Content Consultant:
Betty L. Carlan
Research Librarian
International Motorsports Hall of Fame
Talladega, Alabama

Capstone press

Mankato, Minnesota

Blazers is published by Capstone Press,
151 Good Counsel Drive, P.O. Box 669, Mankato, Minnesota 56002.
www.capstonepress.com

Library of Congress Cataloging-in-Publication Data
Riley, Gail Blasser.
    NASCAR training ground / by Gail Blasser Riley.
    p. cm. — (Blazers. The World of NASCAR)
    Includes bibliographical references and index.
    ISBN-13: 978-1-4296-1284-5 (hardcover)
    ISBN-10: 1-4296-1284-3 (hardcover)
    1. Stock car racing — United States — Juvenile literature. 2. Automobile
racing — Training — United States — Juvenile literature. 3. NASCAR
(Association) — Juvenile literature. I. Title. II. Series.
GV1029.9.S74R57 2008
796.72 — dc22   2007029965

Summary: Describes NASCAR's second series, also known as the NASCAR
    Nationwide Series, including the series history, drivers, and tracks.

Essential content terms are **bold** and are defined on the spread where they
first appear.

Editorial Credits
Mandy Robbins, editor; Bobbi J. Wyss, designer; Jo Miller, photo researcher

Photo Credits
AP Images, 11, 13; James Crisp, 6
Brian Cleary/www.bcpix.com, 12
Corbis/Icon SMI/Worth Canoy, 16–17, 26; Reuters/Harry Reiter, 20–21;
    The Sharpe Image/Sam Sharpe, 18
Getty Images for NASCAR/Andy Lyons, 5, 8–9; Chris Graythen, 25; Dilip
    Vishwanat, cover; Jonathan Ferrey, 14–15, 28–29; Robert Laberge, 23;
    Getty Images, Inc./Harry How, 27; Jonathan Ferrey, 22

1 2 3 4 5 6 13 12 11 10 09 08

Table of Contents

Edwards Upset

Racing fans filled the Kentucky Speedway on June 16, 2007, for the Meijer 300. Carl Edwards had a big lead.

start of 2007, Meijer 300

5

But on lap 157, Edwards' car crashed coming out of a pit stop. Suddenly, it was anyone's race. Running in third place, Stephen Leicht saw his chance to win.

Carl Edwards leading Meijer 300

With 12 laps to go, Brad Coleman's number 18 car was the only car in Leicht's way. Leicht passed Coleman on the outside.

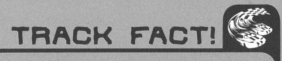

TRACK FACT!

From 1984 to 2007, the second series was called the Busch Series. In 2008, the name changed to the NASCAR Nationwide Series.

Leicht crossing the finish line

Leicht raced his hardest for the last 10 laps. When the checkered flag waved, Leicht had his first second series win.

TRACK FACT!

By 2007, Carl Edwards had driven in 99 Busch Series races. He won 13 of them.

History of the Series

NASCAR's second series has been around since 1950. Young drivers have always driven in the second series to get experience.

Convertible stock car race, 1956

11

Until 1982, different parts of the country held their own second series races. In 1982, NASCAR combined all of these series into one.

1983, Dale Earnhardt wins second series race.

13

Today, the NASCAR second series is a big hit. Races are held all over the United States. The first *international* race was held in Mexico City in 2005.

Autodromo Hermanos Rodriguez, Mexico City

international — including more than one country

Second Series Car

headlight decals

front air dam

16

rear wing

roll cage

2006, Arizona Travel 200

18

Series Drivers

Through many changes,
one thing has stayed the same.
The second series is where
drivers prove their skill.

Drivers master the second series before racing in the **_Sprint Cup_** series. Second series races often include wild crashes. Young drivers take daring chances in these races.

Sprint Cup — the highest level series in NASCAR racing

Older drivers race in the second series too. Mark Martin has raced in the Sprint Cup series for 25 years. In that time, he also won 47 second series races.

Mark Martin

Carl Edwards

Drivers like Martin and Carl Edwards race in both series. Many fans think it's unfair for Sprint Cup drivers to race in the second series.

Training Ground Tracks

Each second series race is exciting and different. Many differences have to do with the racetracks.

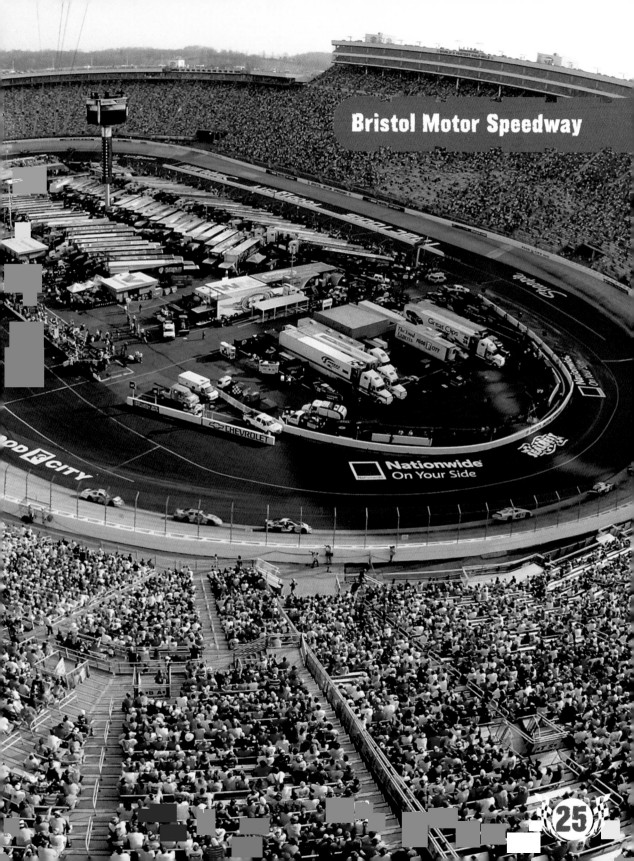

Bristol Motor Speedway

25

Some tracks are long and wide.
The California Speedway is 2 miles
(3.2 kilometers) long and wider than most
tracks. Cars race five-wide on this track.

The Bristol Motor Speedway is called the world's fastest half mile. This short track has steep **banks**. Cars race close together and crash a lot.

bank — the angle of a track

Bristol Motor Speedway

Mexico City has a road course. It runs 2.5 miles (4 kilometers) and has many turns. Wherever a race is held, fans expect exciting racing action from NASCAR's second series.

Autodromo Hermanos Rodriguez

The road course in Mexico City is called Autodromo Hermanos Rodriguez. It means the Rodriguez Brothers racetrack.

Glossary

bank (BANGK) — the angle of the track; if a track has a high bank, the top of the track is much higher than the bottom of the track.

front air dam (FRUNT AIR DAM) — a body panel in the front of a car that cuts wind turbulence and creates a smoother ride

international (in-tur-NASH-uh-nuhl) — including more than one nation

rear wing (REER WING) — a wing-shaped part attached to the back of a stock car that helps improve the car's handling

second series (SEH-kund SIH-rees) — NASCAR's minor league stock car racing series; the second series is like minor league baseball except that athletes from the top series are allowed to compete; from 1984 to 2007 it was called the Busch Series.

Sprint Cup (SPRINT CUP) — the championship held in NASCAR's top stock car racing series; from 2004 to 2007, it was called the Nextel Cup; from 1972 through 2003, it was called the Winston Cup; before 1972, it was known as the Grand National.

Read More

Kelley, K. C., and Bob Woods. *Young Stars of NASCAR.* Pleasantville, New York: Reader's Digest, 2005.

Savage, Jeff. *Jeff Gordon.* Amazing Athletes. Minneapolis: Lerner, 2007.

Sherman, Josepha. *Dale Earnhardt Jr.* Robbie Readers. Hockessin, Del.: Mitchell Lane, 2005.

Internet Sites

FactHound offers a safe, fun way to find Internet sites related to this book. All of the sites on FactHound have been researched by our staff.

Here's how:
1. Visit *www.facthound.com*
2. Choose your grade level.
3. Type in this book ID **1429612843** for age-appropriate sites. You may also browse subjects by clicking on letters, or by clicking on pictures and words.
4. Click on the **Fetch It** button.

FactHound will fetch the best sites for you!

Index